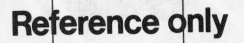

Reference only

Roland Holloway's
NORTHAMPTONSHIRE

Fifty years of photographs

1924–1974

Northamptonshire Libraries

Published by

NORTHAMPTONSHIRE LIBRARIES

27 Guildhall Road, Northampton NN1 1EF

ISBN 0 905391 10 1

Designed by Bernard Crossland
Typeset in Melior 10 on 11pt
and printed in Great Britain by
Stanley L. Hunt (Printers) Ltd, Midland Road,
Rushden, Northamptonshire

ACKNOWLEDGEMENTS
Northamptonshire Libraries are grateful to the
Northampton *Chronicle and Echo* for permission to
reproduce photographs from the Roland Holloway
Collection, and to the *Tatler* magazine for permission
to reproduce illustrations 206, 226 and 245
Several other illustrations have also been
reproduced from photogravure or half-tone
reproductions, but the original publications in which
they appeared have not been traced

FRONTISPIECE

Northampton: Christmas decorations and All Saints Church,
seen from Gold Street

ENDPAPERS

Front: Maypole dancing at Harpole (illustration 281)
Back: Towcester races (illustration 208)

CONTENTS

Figures are picture numbers

FOREWORD

*My father always asserted that in 1905 he had two
infants — the* Independent *which he founded, and
myself . . . it was certainly not conjectured then that
I was to be associated with the journal for over
half a century.*

Roland Holloway

'Roly' Holloway's contribution to the historical record of Northampton, and the County, is unique.

In a career which touched six decades he covered some 28,000 assignments, first for the *Northampton Independent* which was founded by his father, and then for the *Chronicle and Echo*, from which he retired in October 1970.

He has left behind a selection of the 80,000 photographs he took during that time — of royalty, of murderers, of events of great national rejoicing and mourning, some of which are reproduced in this book. They are a fitting memorial and tribute to a man who, in his time, was the best known face in town.

A press photographer's life, though, is not always glamorous and full of drama. There are lesser, routine events to cover — the summer fête, the garden party, and all the other functions which are unlikely to produce a startling news picture but are vitally important to all the people directly involved. It is a measure of the professionalism of the man that Roly would bring to bear on each and every assignment the same qualities of photographic craftsmanship, charm and courtesy which helped him to record some of the most memorable moments in our town's history.

He disdained the equipment modern photography had to offer towards the end of his career, and preferred to rely on his large but trusty plate camera. It is plain from the pages of this book that it did not let him down.

I met Roly for the first time in 1959 and recall with appreciation the occasions when the worldly-wise newspaperman with already more than thirty years experience would bale out the sixteen-year-old raw trainee reporter when we went out together on jobs which, to me at any rate, were tough events to cover.

He never lost his willingness to help the new recruits to journalism, and foolish were those who chose to ignore the quiet advice of the veteran professional.

A self-effacing character, Roly was a regular visitor to the new offices of the *Chronicle and Echo* during his retirement, which came before the newspaper moved from its old premises on the Market Square.

All of us at the *Chronicle and Echo* who knew him, and the thousands of people in the town and county who, at one time or another, came in his sights, will miss Roly. But his photographs remain, a permanent testimony to his skill and to his remarkable career.

PHILIP GREEN, Editor, *Chronicle and Echo.*

1. The young press photographer outside the offices of the *Northampton Independent* in St Giles' Street, Northampton. He sits astride a DOT motorcycle, with oil-cooled engine; it has a 'bullet' side-car.

2. Roland Holloway was a member of the National Fire Service during the Second World War. Here he is seen on a Royal Enfield machine.

'Pop to my younger brother and me'

Roland, 'Pop' to my younger brother and me, was devoted to his job as a press photographer. His working day usually meant long hours away from home and his family saw very little of him during his early years. He will be remembered by many for his trilby hat and camera case, and most families of 'old' Northampton will at some time have encountered Roland, whether it be at their wedding, a dance, rally, sports occasion or scores of other activities covered by the local paper. This commitment to his work now provides its dividends for those of us he has left behind.

GORDON HOLLOWAY

EDITORIAL NOTE

Roland Holloway was a remarkable photographer. First and foremost he was the complete professional, willing to go anywhere at any time in order to cover an important event; often he could be seen perched perilously on buildings or monuments in order to obtain a good shot. More than this, he had a keen sense of design and pattern which make many of his photographs, even those taken for routine occasions, a delight to the eye. He was known as 'King of the kids' for the skill with which he photographed children, and the manner in which he was able to capture their laughter and enthusiasm. It is an aspect of his art which is demonstrated time and again in this book. He was also 'almost' a society photographer, in that his high quality portraits of the celebrated were much in demand by such magazines as the *Tatler* and the *Sketch*.

Although his work was mainly concerned with the Northampton area, occasionally an important event or the visit of a famous personality would take him further afield. We consequently make no apology for including a number of 'out of the County' photographs. Unfortunately many of the 80,000 photographs he took have been lost or damaged, whilst others remain only in the form of rough half-tone or photogravure prints. Some of these have nevertheless been included where they include places or personalities of particular interest.

Most of the text for this book was completed by Roland Holloway before his death, but some additions and revisions have proved necessary in order to bring

the work to a conclusion. In general titles and forms of address are those in use at the time a particular photograph was taken, though exceptions are made where this could lead to difficulties in identifying individuals.

On some half-a-dozen occasions, photographs by other photographers have been included where they help to identify the location of Roland Holloway's own photographs. In each case the source is given in brackets following the caption.

3. Roland Holloway pictured after his retirement, holding his trusty plate camera.

CHANGING NORTHAMPTON

THE TOWN CENTRE

4. Northampton Market Square from the North.

5. Northampton Market Square in the 1950s. For centuries the *Peacock Hotel* was a main feature of Northampton Market Square, and in its early days was a noted coaching inn with stabling for over thirty horses. The balcony also served as a 'platform' for political, religious and other speakers. A deed of 1456 records that a hospital called the 'pecock' was sold and the subsequent hotel erected which in turn was sold for £22, the purchaser being the King's Lieutenant and Mayor! All was demolished in 1960-61 under the re-development scheme. The Peacock Way shopping precinct now stands on part of the site.

8. *Below.* Like nearby Conduit Lane, Drum Lane has been used by pedestrians as a shortcut for hundreds of years. In earlier times it was called *Drury Lane* which lapsed into *The Drums* before the present one. It has changed little over the years; still dominating the skyline at one end is the tower of All Saints Church. What was an old inn is now the *Rifle Drum* whilst opposite is an entrance to 'Shipman's' (officially the *White Hart*) founded in 1782.

7. The jetty called Conduit Lane connecting Mercers' Row with the Market Square. For centuries it was known as *The Gutt*—another form of the word gutter. To prevent rubbish being deposited in it a gate was put up at each end in 1745. The present name derives from the *Great Conduit* built about 1481 on the Market Square. There was also a *Little Conduit* (built about 1300) in front of All Saints Church.

6. *Opposite.* Northampton Market Square during an evening in the early 1930s when members of the band of the 2nd Battalion, Northamptonshire Regiment beat retreat as part of an annual Regimental Cricket Week activities programme. A large crowd assembled to watch the fifty minute marching spectacle.

9. A clean up in operation for the fourteen large canopied statues which are a feature of Northampton Town Hall façade.

10. The Court buildings of Sessions House in George Row were completed in 1678. The architect was probably Henry Bell, who was concerned with the re-building of All Saints Church after 1675.

11. *Below*. Every year when a new mayor of Northampton is elected his name is added to those of many of his predecessors which, with the appropriate date, are inscribed on small shields hanging in an upstairs corridor at the Town Hall. They go back to 1377, but the history of the office goes back to 1189 when Richard I granted the town its first charter, giving Northampton the right to elect a mayor. Among the shields are two picked out in red bearing the name Lawrence Washington, an ancestor of American president George Washington, who held office in 1533 and 1546.

12. A view from the balcony of All Saints Church in the 1930s at mid-morning, showing the junction of Gold Street, Bridge Street and The Drapery. The traffic consisted of two open-deck trams, three cars and a bicycle. Pedestrians proceed casually across the entrance to George Row.

13. Northampton's last electric tram leaves Mercers' Row for the depot at midnight in December 1934. On board were civic representatives and their wives including, left, Councillor Ralph Smith and the Mayor, Alderman A. Burrows. On the right is Chief Constable John Williamson. Standing at the far end are Councillor A. L. Chown, chairman of the Transport Committee who drove the tram, and John Cameron, transport manager.

14. They were cheerful men, the workers who cleaned Northampton's trams when they came 'home to roost' at St. James' End. They 'clocked in' at 11.30 p.m., and left after an early breakfast in their own canteen at 2 a.m.

15. On guard outside All Saints Church during a service attended by the judge, prior to the opening of Northamptonshire Assizes.

POST WAR
REDEVELOPMENT:
THE BEGINNING

16. The widening of Abington Street in 1946.

17. Workmen go aloft during demolition for road widening at the bottom of Abington Street in 1946.

18. Wareings' slipper factory on Abington Square was an early victim of modernisation.

19. Kerr Street, along with others leading to the Police and Fire stations, vanished in 1972.

20. Private and other premises in Wood Street reduced to rubble in 1971. Also awaiting their fate are Birdsall's bookbinding works on the right, and the Fanciers Working Men's Club on the left.

21

22

21. Wood Street. A view from the same spot a few months later as Northampton House begins to arise.

22. Old and new on the Mounts. Northampton House towers over the former Randall's shoe factory. The new Lady's Lane now runs along the site.

23. Northampton House on completion in 1973, alongside the former Fanciers Working Men's Club in Wood Street. Built at a cost of £2,000,000, and standing twelve storeys high, it is the town's highest building. It had a mixed reception on completion being described as 'vulgar', 'a visual disaster' and 'the biggest contribution to the despoilation of the town'.

24. Clouds over the Market Square. The crane indicates that work has begun on the building of Barclaycard's offices in Marefair.

25. The site of the present Barclaycard offices in Marefair. Buildings on the right include the *North Western Hotel* and Grose's garage.

26. A view from the other end of Marefair shows the newly erected Barclaycard offices. The shops in the foreground were demolished and later replaced by an office block. Chalk Lane is on the left.

27. The Lotus factory and office in Victoria Street, August 1973. This view was only made possible by the demolition of the houses opposite. Lotus Ltd, the shoe manufacturing firm, was founded in 1832 and is now located at new premises in Weedon Road.

28. The Lotus factory was demolished in 1974.

29. Lady's Lane from Newland.

30. Lady's Lane, looking towards Sheep Street in October, 1973.

31. Premises at the bottom of Sheep Street as they appeared prior to 1974.

32. Once elegant town houses at the bottom of Sheep Street are now a block of offices.

33-4. Lower Mounts: above in 1972 and below in October 1973

35. Great Russell Street looking from east to west as it appeared in 1974 before demolition. At the bottom of the 'longest street without a turning' is twelve-storey Northampton House completed two years earlier. Part of the *Chronicle and Echo* offices now occupy the bottom corner site.

36. Upper Mounts and Great Russell Street corner with the *Town Arms* pub—the site of the new *Chronicle and Echo* offices.

THE MAKING OF THE GROSVENOR CENTRE

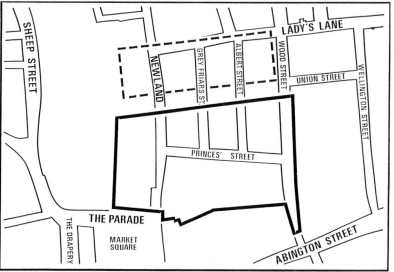

37. The Market Square entrance to the Grosvenor Centre with the new Welsh House on the right (*Chronicle and Echo*).

39. *Opposite, top.* This is how premises on The Parade looked before 1972 when parking was allowed on the Market Square. It is doubtful if any one event caused such controversy as the demise of the Emporium Arcade (centre).

38. ▬▬▬ Area covered by the Grosvenor Shopping Centre, opened in July 1975.
▬ ▬ ▬ Area covered by the Greyfriars 'bus station, opened in April 1976.

39. (*continued*) There was a 'save the arcade' crusade with a petition of over 10,000 signatures. A public enquiry was held, letters to the press flooded in, councillors were lobbied, the M.P. consulted, a deputation went to the Department of the Environment, and even the national Victorian Society took the matter up—all to no avail; now Boots the Chemists dominates the site. Alongside was Abel's music shop, a very old established firm which ceased trading with the re-development. The glass and china firm of Church's was later installed in the reconstructed Welsh House; the newspaper office was transferred to the Mounts. A plaque on the wall of its former site (now *C & A's*) reads 'Founded in 1720, the *Northampton Mercury* was printed here from 1730 to 1978. Home of the *Daily Echo*, now the *Chronicle and Echo* from 1880 to 1978.' The Leicester Building Society, part of which is shown on the left, moved out and returned after reconstruction.

40. The Market Square in 1972.

41. A view across the Market Square in 1973. The former *Chronicle and Echo* offices stand in isolation on The Parade while the giant cranes work on the early stages of the Grosvenor Centre complex.

42. The bottom of Newland (now the Grosvenor Centre) showing part of the former Temperance Hall cinema, one of the oldest surviving cinemas in the country. In 1964 it became a bingo hall before closing. Next to it is a Grade 2 listed building, a shop and a taxi garage.

43. The same view after demolition.

44. Looking up Newland in 1972.

45. The top of Newland, looking towards the Market Square in August, 1973.

46. A reminder of the area to the West of the Police and Fire stations in the 1930s.

47. A tree in the gardens in Newland defies destruction—but only for a time.

48. In the final stages of demolition is Princes' Street Baptist Church. It was built over a century ago when a section of the congregation of College Street Church disagreed over a matter of policy and decided to build a 'breakaway' church.

49. The corner of Abington Street and Wood Street in 1972.

50. Another view of Wood Street in 1972.

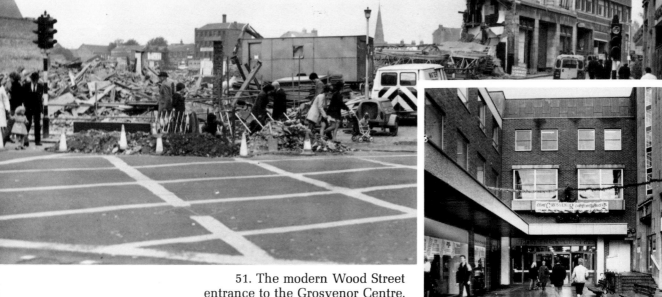

51. The modern Wood Street entrance to the Grosvenor Centre. (*Northamptonshire Libraries*)

52. Welsh House in 1831 when it accommodated the offices of the *Northampton Herald*. The house was one of the few town centre properties to escape the Great Fire of 1675. The arms are those of the Parker family, one of whom, Samuel Parker, became Bishop of Oxford in 1686 (*Northamptonshire Libraries*).

53. This view in 1972 shows Welsh House without the original gables. On the left is Newland, now the Market Square entrance to the Grosvenor Centre.

55. Welsh House, June 1973.

54. The unusual heraldic sign. The inscription in Welsh reads 'Without God, without everything, with God enough'.

56. Welsh House, August 1973.

57. Welsh House, June 1984. (*Chronicle and Echo*)

A MISCELLANY OF BUILDINGS

58. For many years the name of Derngate was associated with the United Counties 'bus station, seen here before demolition in order to make way for the £10,000,000 Leisure Centre to rise on the site which has given the name not only local but national importance. Meanwhile the green United Counties 'buses mingle with the Corporation red, operating from the 'bus station adjacent to the Grosvenor Centre.

59. Notre Dame convent school, Abington Street was demolished in 1979.

60. Former brewery buildings in Bridge Street. On the left is the original Northampton Brewery Company's building; the corner building was built for Watney's 'Red Barrel' production in 1961 at a cost of £1,000,000. Both buildings are now demolished.

61. A view up Gold Street showing the *Queen's Head Hotel*. The hotel suffered damage during the war when a bomb lodged there following the crash of a Stirling bomber in Gold Street. It was demolished in 1961.

62. Aquila House was the first home of Barclaycard before it moved to purpose-built premises in Marefair. It was demolished and replaced by a new Aquila House in 1985.

63. The *Grand Hotel* in Gold Street when the old 'Dolphin Bar' existed.

64. The old Midland Bank on Wood Hill. It was demolished to make way for an enlarged Midland Bank which was opened in January 1968.

65. The old Gas Company offices in Abington Street. They were demolished to make way for Marks and Spencer's store, opened in 1969.

66. The offices of the Liberal Club in Castilian Street. The building is now Knight's Club.

67. The Friendly Societies' Club and Institute on the Mounts. The site was later occupied by part of the *Chronicle and Echo* offices.

68. St. Edmund's Church in Wellingborough Road. It was demolished in 1980.

69. This dilapidated garage was formerly Commercial Street Congregational Church.

70. The Arts Theatre Club in Pytchley Street, now used as the Ukrainian Club.

71. Phipps' baths in Cattle Market Road, the building where many Northamptonians learned to swim. It was demolished in 1937.

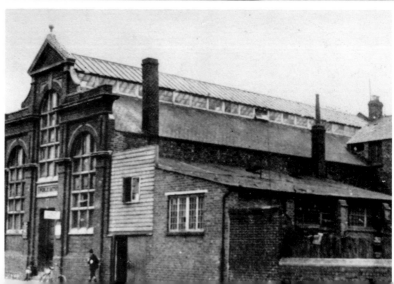

RURAL NORTHAMPTON

72. Misty morning in Thornton Park, Northampton.

73. Kingsthorpe Park, often known as Thornton Park, was acquired by the Corporation in 1938 from the Thornton family. The house with gardens of some fifteen acres lies just off the main Market Harborough Road leaving Northampton. It was not until 1939 that the parkland was opened to the public.

Kingsthorpe Hall is a typical eighteenth-century neo-classical building of about 1774, and was used as offices for the former Estates Department after their transfer from Abington Park. The building is now a Community Centre for various local groups and also a Children's Day Centre.

74. The circular staircase at Kingsthorpe Hall.

75. Hopeful signs of a good crop of fruit and rhubarb for this gardener on his Cliftonville allotment, one of many situated just off the Bedford Road. All have now disappeared and been replaced by a garage, filling station and industrial buildings.

76. Autumn in Abington Park.

77. Eastfield Park shortly after it was taken over by the Corporation in 1952. Previously it was part of property owned by the Manfield family of Weston House, while another part belonged to the Ray family who lived at Eastfield House.

78. Residents of Eastfield Estate enjoy the nearby lake in Eastfield Park.

79. Young 'mothers' in Abington Park.

80. The most central and conspicuous of the town's open spaces is Becket's Park. For centuries the area was known as Cow Meadow. The present name derives from nearby historic Becket's Well. In the early 1920s, to help relieve unemployment following the First World War, improvements were made by levelling some undulating ground and the construction of a lake.

81. Fishermen in Becket's Park.

82. Crocus time in Dallington vicarage garden. It is now the site of council houses.

83. A magnolia tree in Abington Park.

84. Blossom time in 1950 at Dallington Green.

85. Kingsthorpe Church from the bottom of Mill Lane, before modern road improvements changed the scene.

WARTIME AND THE
YEARS OF AUSTERITY

86. Gas mask testing, 1939.

87. Work in progress in Sheep Street, Northampton where kerb stones were painted white at intervals to pin point their positions during the 'Blackout'.

88. Car bumpers were painted white in the war time 'Blackout' to assist drivers and pedestrians. Note the masked headlamps.

89. A Civil Defence messenger brings orders to the Home Guard in Bridge Street, Northampton, during a combined exercise. There were 750 concrete road blocks in Northampton, intended as obstructions to enemy tanks.

90. A Home Guard parade on Northampton Market Square in October 1940. On the right is Welsh House.

91. Tank training in what later became the grounds of Cherry Orchard School, Weston Favell.

92. A.T.S. 'red caps' in a Northampton billet.

93. Armoured car inspection.

94. Schoolboys investigate a tank on Northampton Market Square during War Weapons Week, November 1940.

95. Collecting for the *Chronicle and Echo* fund for the troops at the Lotus shoe factory.

96. Congestion on Northampton Market Square in the early 1940s.

97-8. Early in the last war a contingent of Canadian Division troops were billeted in Northampton and during a spell of hot weather they took a dip in Midsummer Meadow open air baths. They were to see service in the ill-fated Dieppe raid in August 1942, which resulted in 3,379 casualties out of a Canadian force of 5,100. The baths were demolished in 1983 as part of local government cuts in expenditure.

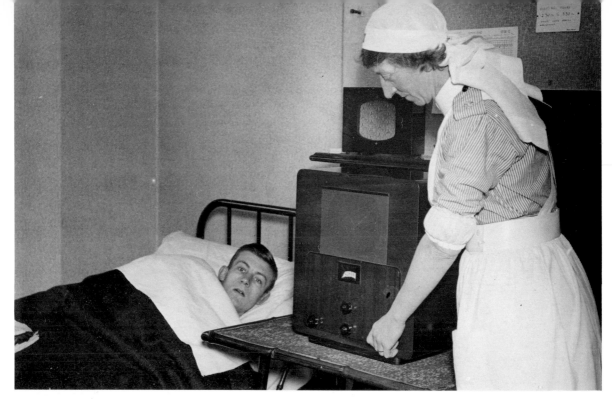

99. Cheering the sick soldiers. One of the wireless sets which were installed in military hospitals by the *Chronicle and Echo* Comforts Fund.

100. A lone bomb dropped at Weston Favell landed in an open space. Here children search for souvenirs among the debris.

101. Northampton Drill Hall was built in 1859 at a cost of £7,000 and originally contained dwellings for twenty-four army personnel one of whom caused a sensation by murdering two of his comrades.

102. *Above, right.* After the Second World War the Drill Hall became a 'demob' centre.

103. 'Demobbed' men leave the Drill Hall with boxes containing their 'demob' or 'civvy' suits.

104. The Freedom of the Borough of Northampton is conferred on the Northamptonshire Regiment, 8th June 1946.

105. A corner of Delapre Estate where aluminium 'prefabs' were built. Others were built in Bants Lane. They were erected at the rate of five a day.

106. The war had been over for two years but labour shortages and extreme weather conditions combined to produce a fuel crisis throughout Britain in early 1947. Electricity supplies were cut and people shivered in unheated homes. Some found relief by using coke instead of coal and there were long queues at Northampton Gas Works as people waited to fill up old prams, trolleys and sacks.

107. This is not a wartime scene in the blackout, but a section of Abington Street in Northampton on an early evening during a power cut in 1947, taken with a three minute exposure.

108. A corridor in Northampton Town Hall during a power cut in 1947.

ROYALTY

109. Queen Mary and Earl Spencer in the doorway of Sulgrave Manor. The Queen requested that a complete set of photographs of the visit should be sent to Buckingham Palace saying that they would be 'a welcome addition to Her Majesty's album, being as they are, varied and delightful sets of wonderfully clear and good photographs'.

110. Coinciding with Queen Mary's visit to Sulgrave was a garden fête at Great Brington which she attended. She is seen here watching a dancing display together with young Viscount Althorp, the present Earl and father of the Princess of Wales, the late Earl Spencer and the Rector of Great Brington, the Reverend J. B. King.

111. A group photograph taken in May 1938, when Queen Mary spent a weekend at Boughton House as the guest of the Duke and Duchess of Buccleuch who are seen seated on either side of her. Also in the house-party were, from the left: the Duchess of Northumberland; Lady Caroline Scott, younger daughter of the hosts; and Lady Baldwin. Standing: Lord Henry Scott; Commander Hawkins; the Right Honourable W. Ormsby-Gore, Colonial Secretary; Mr David Scott; the Right Honourable Sir Francis Lindley; Lady Margaret Hawkins; Lady Constance Milnes Gaskell (Lady in Waiting); Lady Beatrice Ormsby-Gore; and Lord Baldwin, a former Prime-Minister.

112. For the visit of the Prince of Wales in 1927 to Sears' shoe factory in Northampton, Roland Holloway had visited the factory earlier and focused his camera on a substitute standing on a chalk line which can just be seen in the photograph. When the Prince saw the line, he called his entourage together with the remark: 'Come on, we must toe the line,' which they all did. From left to right: Councillor and Mrs James Peach, Mr W. T. Sears, the Prince, Chief Constable John Williamson, and Mr F. W. Panther.

113. A specially posed group at Northampton Castle Station in May, 1930, when the Duke of York (later King George VI) arrived for an official visit. With him from the left are: the Mayor, Councillor Ralph Smith; Alderman W. Harvey-Reeves; Alderman S. S. Campion; Alderman A. E. Ray, Deputy Mayor; Mr J. T. Bentham, Stationmaster; Colonel C. L. Malone M.P.; the Chief Constable, John Williamson, and the Town Clerk, Mr W. R. Kew. It was Northampton Festival Week, and the Duke opened a manufacturers' trades exhibition and attended a week-long pageant and carnival.

114. In May 1958, the Duchess of Gloucester (later Princess Alice) opened the new head-quarters of the Women's Institute in Albion Place, Northampton. Presenting the bouquet is Fiona Macdonald-Buchanan with assistance from her grandmother, the Hon. Mrs Macdonald-Buchanan, the County President.

115. The Duchess of Gloucester shares a joke after opening Barton Seagrave Hall, 'Fellow-ship House', a home for the aged.

116. Princess Elizabeth leaves a first aid tent at the opening of Grendon Hall Youth Club in 1946. Holding open the flap is the Chief Constable of North-amptonshire, Captain R. H. D. Bolton.

117. Princess Elizabeth inspects a guard-of-honour of the Northamptonshire
Regiment drawn up on Spencer Parade when she visited Northampton General
Hospital in July 1946. With her is Major C. J. M. Watts. They are followed by
the late Earl Spencer.

118. *Left.* Princess Elizabeth acknowledges cheers outside the Barratt Maternity Home in Northampton as she leaves after a visit to the General Hospital in 1946.

119. The Queen with her host, Lieutenant-Colonel P. Phillips, arriving at Thorpe Lubenham church for morning service, following an official visit to Leicester.

120. Cheering schoolgirls get smiles and waves from the Queen and Prince Philip during their visit to Corby and Stamford in 1961.

121. In May 1950 Princess Margaret spent a weekend at Althorp as guest of Earl and Countess Spencer, during which she attended a Sunday morning service at Great Brington. The Chief Constable of Northamptonshire, Captain R. H. D. Bolton, stands by the door as she leaves the church.

122. Pytchley Hunt Ball at Holdenby House in 1951. Princess Margaret is greeted by Major Peter Borwick, M.F.H., with centre, the Honourable Mrs J. G. Lowther, and on the right, Captain and Mrs George Lowther (hosts).

123. The Duke and Duchess of Gloucester held a family party at Barnwell Manor in November 1960 to celebrate their silver wedding anniversary. They are seen leaving the Manor for a Sunday morning service at the nearby church. Following the Duke and Duchess are the Princess Royal, an aunt of the Queen, right, Princess Alice of Athlone, Prince William, Prince Richard (the present Duke) right, and Sir Godfrey Thomas.

124. The Queen with Prince Charles and Princess Anne
on their way to Thorpe Lubenham church for Sunday morning service
in March, 1956. Following are Lieutenant Colonel Phillips,
his children, Mrs Phillips and Prince Philip.

COUNTRY HOUSES
AND FAMILIES

125. Captain and Mrs G. E. Belville and their daughters at the ornate Victorian entrance porch to Fermyn Woods Hall, near Kettering in 1932. The Captain had a distinguished army career and was a Master of the Woodland Pytchley Hunt from 1920 to 1932. When the family moved from the Hall the new owner decided to reduce its size and many of the twenty-nine bedrooms were dispensed with, together with furniture and other items. Part of the building included in the auction sale was the elaborate fifteen-feet wide porch seen here.

126. A family group at Watford Court, a fine stone-built mansion dating back to 1568, situated near Long Buckby. The photograph was taken in 1932 and shows Lord and Lady Henley with their three daughters, Barbara, Griselda and Nancy. Lord Henley was chairman of Northamptonshire County Council, while Lady Henley was a temperance worker and Women's Institute champion.

127. Billing Hall, the home of the Elwes family *(from a postcard)*.

128. A group taken in 1931 when Lady Winefride Elwes, seated in centre, held a family re-union at her Billing Hall home.

Lady Winefride's own children are standing from left: Mr Simon Elwes, the celebrated portrait painter who numbered royalty among his sitters; Monsignor Valentine Elwes, former private secretary to Cardinal Hinsley (Archbishop of Westminster) and a privy Chamberlain to the Pope. He became a Royal Navy chaplain during the Second World War and five of his six brothers rose to the rank of Colonel; Captain Rudolph Elwes, Miss Margaret Elwes, Major Geoffrey Elwes, Miss Clare Elwes, Mr Guy Elwes and Mr Richard Elwes (later Sir Richard) who was appointed Recorder for Northampton in 1946, later becoming a High Court judge. His daughter, Polly, won an award for the best Television female personality.

Seated from left are: Mrs H. deBless (aunt), Mrs Rudolph Elwes, Lady Winefride, Mrs Geoffrey Elwes, Mrs Richard Elwes and Mrs Guy Elwes. Father of the family was Mr Gervase Elwes a celebrated tenor killed in America in 1921. The stately eighteenth-century mansion with its verdant lawns and huge cedar and beech trees was demolished in 1956. Now the area is a residential estate with two roads named after the family.

129.
An impressive
Corpus Christi
procession for a
service in the
grounds of
Billing Hall.

130. The first Lord Hesketh, grandfather of the present Lord, in the stately mansion at Easton Neston, Towcester. Included are some art treasures, a fine tapestry, antique furniture and ornaments. Formerly Sir Thomas Fermor-Hesketh, he received the elevation in 1935 for political and public services in Northamptonshire. He was also Chairman of the Board of Governors of the General Hospital, High Sheriff, President of the League of Nations and founder-Chairman of Towcester Racecourse. The mansion was built by Nicholas Hawksmoor in the Italian style; the manor came into the Fermor family in 1528 and has remained with descendants ever since.

131. Lord Hesketh, with his daughters, Louise, left and Flora in the garden of Easton Neston, Towcester.

132. Major the Hon. John Fermor-Hesketh and his bride-to-be Miss Patricia Macaskie Cole beside one of the massive Chinese bronzes that adorn the drawing-room at Easton Neston, Towcester.

133. A smile from the bride as she signs the register at their London wedding in 1946. The witnesses were Lord Hesketh, left (his brother), Miss Antonia Izod and Mr F. S. G. Underwood.

134. The late Sir Gyles Isham and his faithful dog pose in 1969 among some of the valuable paintings in Lamport Hall. He was the last Isham to live there after more than four hundred years of occupation by the family. When he died in 1976 he left the Hall and its contents to the Lamport Hall Trust which now owns, maintains and opens it to support education and the arts. Sir Gyles, a bachelor, served in the King's Royal Rifle Corps rising to the rank of Lieutenant Colonel and was a noted Shakespearean actor, appearing both at home and in America where he also had a part in a Greta Garbo film.

135-6. Burghley House has been open to the public since 1798, and there is a visitors' book dating back to 1809 when the then Lady Exeter took people round, giving the fees to charity. The mansion which took twenty-one years to complete is the largest and grandest surviving building of the Elizabethan age, started by William Cecil the first Lord Burghley (1520-1598), and it has been the home of the Cecils and Exeters for over 400 years. The Germans earmarked the mansion for Goering's personal use after they had won the war. The Marquess of Exeter is seen here beside a huge silver wine cooler. In 1928 he had won the 400 metres hurdles Olympics event and two years later the World Hurdles Championship. On the right is the Marchioness.

137. The Queen chats to a huntsman at the gates of Burghley House during a visit in June 1961.

138. Sir Sacheverell Sitwell at Weston Hall near Towcester in the 1960s. Sir Sacheverell was made a Companion of Honour for services to literature, and received the award in a private audience at Buckingham Palace. He was also awarded the Benson Silver Medal by the Royal Society of Literature and was a High Sheriff of Northamptonshire.

139. Deene Park is the Northamptonshire home of Mr and the Hon. Mrs Brudenell; she is the eldest daughter of the late Lord and Lady Dilhorne. The historic Elizabethan mansion has been in the family since 1514 when Sir Robert Brudenell, a Lord Chief Justice, acquired the estate. It included 25 farms subject to a rent of £18 to be paid annually to the Abbey of Westminster. A colourful member of the family was the seventh Earl of Cardigan who led the Charge of the Light Brigade at Balaclava, and relics of this much debated episode can be seen in the house.

140. Beside a fine wrought iron gateway in Holdenby House Gardens, first opened to the public in 1953, are the late Captain and Mrs George Lowther and family. The mansion has many royal associations dating back to Queen Elizabeth I, whose Lord Chancellor Sir Christopher Hatton built the former great palace; at that time it was considered to be the largest private house in the kingdom.

When James I was called from Scotland to occupy the English throne, he and his wife Queen Anne of Denmark stayed at the house. In 1607 the property was ceded back to the Crown. There was also a tragic occasion when Charles I was held captive there for several months following his defeat at the Battle of Naseby in 1645. Cromwell's Parliament ordered the demolition of the vast mansion which was left in ruins apart from portions of the present building, and two handsome outer court stone gateways dated 1583 which are still standing—one of them is visible in the picture. Captain Lowther was a former Joint Master of the Pytchley Hunt, a member of the County Council and the Agricultural Society, a governor of Northampton Grammar School, and Chairman of Kettering Conservative Association.

141-2. The engagement and subsequent wedding in London of Mr John Lowther and Miss Jennifer Bevan.

Mr Lowther, who received the C.B.E. in the Queen's Birthday Honours list in 1983, quit politics after serving on the County Council for fourteen years, latterly as leader of the Conservative group from 1974 to 1984. He became Lord Lieutenant of the County in 1984.

143. Mr Hereward Wake's (now Sir Hereward, 14th Baronet) twenty-first birthday party at Courteenhall in 1937. The photograph shows a family group with his mother and father Major General Sir Hereward Wake (13th Baronet) and Lady Wake, on his right, and his grandmother the Dowager Catherine Lady Wake, on his left. Uncles and Aunts, including Miss Joan Wake, and his brothers and sisters and cousins and Trustees of the Wake Settled Estates are also in the picture—which includes a circular, enlarged inset of Mr Wake.

The celebration lasted three days with a party for all employees and friends on the Courteenhall Estate and a ball in the evening at Courteenhall House.

144. Mr Hereward Wake and his bride, Miss Julia Lees. They were married in London in 1952.

145. The late Marquess of Northampton on his way to a meet of the Oakley Hunt in the late Thirties. In 1965 a crowd of over 300 people converged on Castle Ashby as invited guests to his eightieth birthday celebrations. In a speech of welcome to the tenants, estate workers and friends he recalled that some of the families present had been with the Compton Estates for 300 years. He was a popular chairman of Northamptonshire County Council from 1949 to 1954 and president of the Boys' Brigade for 45 years. In 1958 he married Elspeth Lady Teynham. It was in 1574 that the first Earl Compton began the building and his descendants continued with it until around 1600 when Queen Elizabeth stayed there. King William III was a visitor in 1695 and a dining room is still named after him. He introduced the Dutch custom of planting avenues of trees and the practice was observed for twenty-five years. Like other Elizabethan houses it was built in the shape of the letter E in honour of Queen Elizabeth.

146. The photograph shows a family group. With the Marquess from the left are: Lady Eliza Compton, the Marchioness of Northampton, Lord William Compton, Lady Judith Compton and Earl Compton, the present Lord.

147. Althorp House has been in the possession of the Spencer family for over three hundred years and was opened to the public in 1890. The first owner was knighted by Henry VIII and was recorded as being the biggest sheep breeder in England. In the collections are books dating back to the seventeenth century, valuable items of china, and rare pieces of furniture. But its chief glory is the famous picture gallery which is 115 feet long containing works by the most celebrated artists in the world.

148. The late Earl Spencer
with some of the famous
paintings at Althorp.

149. The late Countess Spencer (grandmother of the Princess of Wales) and Lord Cromwell at a meet of the Pytchley Hunt at Althorp.

PERSONALITIES

150. Labour Prime Minister Clement Attlee and Mrs Attlee pay a visit to Althorp.
On the left is the late Earl Spencer and on the right, the late Duke of Buccleuch.

151. Miss Megan Lloyd George about to sign the visitors' book in the Mayor's Parlour before opening a bazaar in Northampton in 1927. Behind is Alderman S. S. Campion, whose eightieth birthday was about to be celebrated by a dinner.

152. Major Gwilym Lloyd George pauses for a photograph before signing a visitors' book at a function held at Doddridge (Castle Hill) Church in Northampton. Behind him is Chief Constable John Williamson.

153. In 1923 Northampton had its own 'Maggie' when Miss Margaret Bondfield was elected the first Labour M.P. She rose to become the first woman Cabinet minister. Here she acknowledges the crowds during a 1928 visit to the town to give an address in support of Colonel C. L. Malone, walking behind her. Also pictured are Mrs Malone, Alderman A. Burrows and Councillor Mrs A. Adams.

154. A brilliant career in legal and political life was achieved by Lord Dilhorne, formerly Sir Reginald Manningham-Buller, who lived at Greens Norton and died only six months after retirement in 1980 aged 75. Called to the Bar in 1927, he entered Parliament as Conservative member for the Daventry Division in 1943, and became M.P. for South Northamptonshire in 1950. After some years as a barrister he was knighted in 1951 and became Lord High Chancellor in 1962. This photograph was taken at a Conservative rally and fête at Kingsthorpe Hall Park (now Thornton Park) in 1930. With him are his fiancée Lady Mary Lindsay, whom he married shortly afterwards, and on the left Miss Myra Manningham-Buller, his sister.

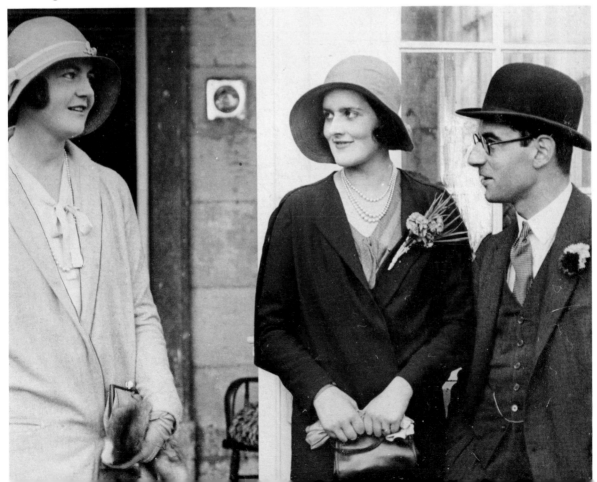

155. A crowd of over 15,000 converged on Boughton House, near Kettering in July 1938: the occasion was a National Government rally addressed by Prime Minister Neville Chamberlain, who was supported by both Labour and Liberal representatives. He spoke of the 'terrible four years of the First World War with its millions of casualties, and doubted that since the world began had there ever been such a spectacle of human madness and folly'.

The photograph shows the Duchess of Buccleuch receiving a bouquet, watched by the Prime Minister and Lady Burghley.

156. Prime Minister Neville Chamberlain delivering his address at the National Government demonstration at Boughton House. Also seen, right to left, are Lord Brassey, Mrs Neville Chamberlain and the Duke of Buccleuch.

157. Robert Maxwell, M.P. for the Buckingham division from 1964 to 1970, with Prime Minister Harold Wilson and Bletchley Council chairman, Jim Cassidy.

158. Sir Keith Joseph, later Minister for Education, stresses a point during his address to members of Northampton Conservative Women's Association in 1970. Also pictured are Cecil Parkinson, prospective Conservative Parliamentary candidate for Northampton, and Mrs A. E. Berrisford, chairman. Mr Parkinson later became Chairman of the Conservative Party.

159. Harold Wilson speaking at Northampton Town Hall in 1964 on behalf of Labour candidate Mr R. T. Paget, later Lord Paget. Lord Paget was Northampton's M.P. from 1945 to 1974.

160. A large gathering of Labour Party supporters attended a celebration dinner held at the former Exeter Hall, Northampton in 1966, marking the twenty-one years as M.P. for the Borough of Reginald Paget, seen centre with his wife. On the left are his old friend Sir Geoffrey de Freitas, M.P. for Kettering and his wife, and on the right Mr George Browett, Chairman of Northampton Labour Party, and Mr George Attwell, agent. An inscribed silver salver was presented to Mr Paget who eventually served twenty-nine years in the Commons before his retirement.

161. During his term of office as Mayor of Northampton in 1924, Councillor H. W. Dover gave a garden party at his St. James' residence for ten of his predecessors.

Seated: from left are Councillor F. G. Parker (1914), Councillor John Woods (1916), Councillor Dover, Councillor T. D. Lewis (1923), Alderman A. J. Chown (1917), whose two sons Arthur and Cyril also became mayors, and Alderman C. Earl (1922).

Standing: Mr G. S. Whiting (1921), Councillor F. Kilby (1919), Councillor W. Harvey-Reeves (1912 and 1920), Mr J. E. Pearse (1915) and Mr J. J. Martin (1918).

162. Two distinguished sons of Northamptonshire photographed in the garden of the Judges' Lodgings adjacent to the Court. Justice (later Sir Richard) Elwes (right) who was the presiding judge on this occasion, was a member of the talented family of Billing Hall. Earlier he had been assistant to famous advocate Norman Birkett in the Rouse murder trial, and was a former Recorder for Northampton. Sir Gyles Isham of Lamport Hall, was High Sheriff; apart from his many interests connected with the County, he was a fine Shakespearean actor.

163. Silver jubilee celebrations of King George V and Queen Mary, May 1935. Deputy Lieutenants of the County in procession to a thanksgiving service in Peterborough Cathedral. From the right are Sir Hereward Wake, Lord Lilford, Lord Brooke, Lord Brassey, Earl Spencer, Alderman S. S. Campion (former Editor of the *Northampton Mercury*) and Brigadier A. F. H. Ferguson.

164-5. For centuries a procession to and from All Saints Church for a short service preceded the opening of Northamptonshire Assizes with the presiding judge in attendance; shown from left to right are Justices Devlin, Stable and Streatfeild.

166. Members of Northampton Town Council at the Armistice Day service in 1966.

167. Former Mayors of Northampton who attended a dinner held at the Wedgwood Restaurant in January, 1965. Front row, from the left, are Alderman E. F. Tompkins (1962), Councillor Mrs E. E. Wilkinson (1960), Councillor J. B. Corrin (the Mayor then in office), Alderman Mrs K. M. Gibbs (1961), and Mr A. W. Lyne (1938). Back row: Alderman A. L. Chown (1940), Alderman J. V. Collier (1954), Mr F. A. Watts (1945), Alderman G. Hackett (1963), Alderman T. H. Cockerill (1956), Alderman W. Lewis (1955), Alderman F. P. Saunders (1957), Alderman C. A. Chown (1950), Mr H. A. Glenn (1939) and Alderman G. Nutt (1959).

168. Pictured at the same function are these Mayoresses: (seated), Mrs C. A. Chown, Mrs A. W. Lyne, Mrs G. Nutt, Mrs F. A. Watts, Mrs E. W. H. Powell, Mrs Percival Williams: (standing), Mrs L. M. Vorse, Miss C. Causebrook, Mrs W. A. Pickering, Mrs T. H. Cockerill, Mrs G. Hackett, Mrs J. B. Corrin, Mrs F. P. Saunders, Mrs J. V. Collier, Miss Barbara Adams, Mrs E. F. Tompkins and Mrs A. L. Chown.

170. World Chief Guide, Olave, Lady Baden-Powell (second from right), meets local Guide leaders at Castle Ashby in 1966.

169. Chief Scout Lord Rowallan walks hand in hand with a Scout Cub during a tour of the camping ground at Northampton Grammar School in 1946.

171. Since it was opened as a museum in 1921, Sulgrave Manor has attracted thousands of visitors every year from all over the world. The picture shows the visit in 1933 of Mr Robert Bingham, the American Ambassador to Britain (centre). With him in a doorway of the Manor are members of the Sulgrave Manor Board, Sir Percy Alden (left) and Sir Harry Brittain, who was actively concerned in the acquisition of Sulgrave Manor to celebrate Anglo-American unity.

172. In June 1938, Flore village had a distinguished visitor in the person of Sir Oliver Lodge, who came to spend his 87th birthday with his son and daughter-in-law Mr and Mrs F. Brodie Lodge at their sixteenth-century Flore House. Sir Oliver was an eminent scientist, inventor and psychic researcher. He held honorary degrees at thirteen universities—Oxford, Cambridge, Manchester, Liverpool, Sheffield, Leeds, Adelaide, Toronto, St. Andrews, Glasgow, Aberdeen, Edinburgh, and Birmingham.

173. To mark his appointment as High Sheriff of Northamptonshire in 1965, Commander and Mrs Derek Lawson held a reception at their home, Passenham Manor near Stony Stratford. The guests included Earl Spencer, then Lord Lieutenant. Commander Lawson later became a Deputy Lieutenant and served as a magistrate for twenty-four years.

174. Miss Mary Bouverie in Delapre Gardens. Miss Bouverie took up residence in Delapre in 1914 and maintained the family tradition of service to the community, being a Justice of the Peace and a prominent member of the Women's Institute. Her death in 1943 marked the passing of the last of the family from Delapre.

175. Miss Joan Wake, the saviour of Delapre Abbey. A decision by Northampton County Borough Council to demolish Delapre was reprieved following much public protest. Joan Wake, secretary of Northamptonshire Record Society, raised in twelve months the £15,000 necessary to restore the building.

176-6a. Mrs. Sophia O'Connor at the age of 102; she died the following year in 1933. She was the aunt of Gervase Elwes, the famous tenor of Billing Hall and also of the Rt. Rev. Dudley Cary Elwes. The gathering in her honour included, back row: Captain Rudolph Elwes, Major Geoffrey Elwes, J.P., and Mgr. Valentine Elwes: (second row), Mr Guy Elwes, Mr Richard Elwes, Mrs Guy Elwes, Mrs Geoffrey Elwes, Mrs Rudolph Elwes and Miss Tindall: (seated), Mrs Walsh, Mrs Tindall, Mrs H. de Bless, Lady Winefride Elwes, Mrs Langford and Mrs Osmaston. Seated on the ground are Miss Prudence and Master Jeremy Elwes.

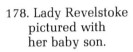
178. Lady Revelstoke
pictured with
her baby son.

177. Lord Revelstoke and
Miss Flora Fermor-Hesketh
were married at the parish
church, Easton Neston
in 1934. Lord Revelstoke
had succeeded his father
earlier that year.

179. Mr Richard Elwes at Billing Hall shortly after being sworn in as Northampton Borough Recorder. With him are his mother (Lady Winefride Elwes) and his wife and children (Ruth and Mark).

180. A charity performance at the Royal Theatre, Northampton. From left to right: the Duchess of Gloucester (later Princess Alice), the Mayor (Alderman Miss Ruth Perkins), the Town Clerk (Mr C. E. Vivian Rowe), Mr R. T. Paget, M.P. (later Lord Paget), Mrs Paget, Lady Hesketh and Sir William Hart, Chairman of Northampton Development Corporation.

181. Sir William and Lady Hart in the grounds of their home Turweston Lodge, near Brackley. Sir William was the first chairman of Northampton Development Corporation.

182. Richard Dimbleby, the well-known broadcaster and television personality, visits the famous model-making firm of Bassett-Lowke in Northampton.

183. Mr John Frisby with his wife and friend on an outing. He lived in an attractive little house in Bedford Place in Northampton, and the horses were stabled at the bottom of Hazelwood Road. At one time he shared stables with his brother Bob at the rear of the Peacock Hotel on Market Square which had been a popular coaching inn. It was demolished in 1960-61 to make way for the present-day Peacock Way shopping precinct. This photograph was used by Mr and Mrs Frisby as a Christmas card in 1939.

184. Jack Train, comedian of 'I.T.M.A.' fame during the war, takes delivery of a new Humber car at Mulliner's in Northampton.

185. Admiration for a fellow photographer from Roland Holloway. Arthur Rice of Wollaston had a national reputation as a photographer of poultry.

186. *Above right.* Trixie Enfield surrounded by her retirement gifts. She was barmaid at the *Plough Hotel* for twenty-five years.

187. Payne, the chimney sweep, would always walk to his engagements followed a few yards away by his son carrying the brushes. They lived in Green Street in a house decorated with hundreds of sea shells, which came into the news when Payne refused to leave under a compulsory purchase order. The house stood in isolation for a long time surrounded by rubble; only after his death was it finally demolished for road widening.

188. A. J. Darnell (Pat), a sportsman-solicitor always wore a top hat and frock coat together with a pipe. He was Borough Coroner for forty years conducting over 4,000 inquests and died a bachelor in 1955 at the age of ninety.

189. It was very rare, if ever, that a foreign ruler or head of state has visited Northampton and not received an official or even unofficial welcome. But such was the case in February 1955 when the then Shah of Iran unexpectedly paid a Sunday morning visit which lasted only about twenty minutes whilst he and a small entourage took refreshments at the Grand Hotel during a tour of Midland horse breeding establishments. The Shah was deposed in January 1979, and died in Egypt in July 1980.

LEISURE AND PLEASURE

190. Children playing in 'happy valley' on the 'Racecourse', Northampton.

191. Hurdles at Northampton Grammar School sports.

192. The pole vault at a school sports at the Northampton British Timken ground, where the first local flood lighting system was installed.

193. Mervyn Williams breaks his Delapre School's senior boys' high jump record at British Timken sports ground.

194.
Northampton
Amateur
Athletic
Club.

195. The
former open
air swimming
pool at
Franklin's
Gardens in
St. James,
Northampton.

196. An escort of fans surround Father T. Aspell as he goes to the starting point of the fathers' race (which he won) at St. Mary's Roman Catholic school sports held on the 'Racecourse', Northampton.

197. The tug-o'-war across the river Ise at Geddington between teams of twenty aside from the north and south sides of the village.

198. Annual outing for inmates of the Northampton Poor Law Institution—or Workhouse as it was commonly known. Sports usually figured in the day's programme and included a tug-o'-war between members of the Board of Guardians and the staff.

199. The meet of Lord Burghley's pack at Althorp in 1939.
The pack was disbanded in 1968.

200. Lord Burghley.

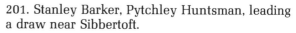

202. *Below*. The Duke of York (later King George VI) and Lady Dalkeith at a Pytchley meet in 1931 at Thornby Grange, where the Duke and Duchess were in residence.

201. Stanley Barker, Pytchley Huntsman, leading a draw near Sibbertoft.

203. Princess Alexandra at Guilsborough for the Pytchley meet in 1955.

204. The Duchess of York (now the Queen Mother) at a meet of the Pytchley Hunt at Thornby Grange in 1931. The pony was for Princess Elizabeth to ride.

205. Mr Ron Mason (trainer-owner) of Guilsborough, with two of his celebrated racehorses.

206. Summer steeplechasing at Towcester in 1936 where the course had just been rebuilt. From left to right: The Hon. Mrs Du Buisson, Sir Hereward Wake, Captain T. G. Du Buisson, Earl and Countess Spencer, Major Warren and Colonel E. G. Warren.

207. View from the grandstand at Towcester racecourse.

208. Towcester races in the Sixties. The racing tradition began when the Empress of Austria rented Easton Neston from the Hesketh family many years ago, and staged a meeting for the benefit of local farmers.

209. A waiting punter at Towcester.

210-11. Thrills and spills at the Grafton Hunter trials in the Thirties.

212. For many years there was a celebrated Army Equitation School at Weedon and this is the team that won many awards both in this country and abroad.

They are from the left: Lt. J. C. H. Mead (R.H.A.), Major Friedberger (R.H.A.), Major J. H. Dudgeon (Scots Greys), Lt. J. A. Talbot-Ponsonby (7th Hussars) and Captain E. D. Howard-Vyse (R.H.A.). Talbot-Ponsonby was killed in the hunting field in 1969 aged sixty-two. He was secretary of the Pytchley, living for a time at Chapel Brampton, and Commanding Officer of the Northamptonshire Yeomanry. It was in show jumping that he became nationally famous having trained Britain's Olympic team which won a gold medal at the Helsinki games in 1952.

213. Polo at Thorpe Lubenham Hall in 1933. For some years regular polo tournaments were held there when it was the home of Sir Harold and Lady Zia Wernher, and Indian Princes often competed. Standing at the rear is Lord Louis Mountbatten.

214. The Maharajah of Kashmir in action.

215. A Pytchley Hunt meet at Sywell Aerodrome in the early 1930s.

216. Northamptonshire Aero Club fancy dress dance at Sywell in 1934. From left to right: Mr R. J. Harrison, Miss S. Mayse, Mr Darrell Moore, Miss Faith Bennett and Mr Charles Bennett, author of 'Blackmail' and other plays.

217. Geoffrey and Jack Linnell, founder members of the Northamptonshire Aero Club.

218. There are many present day aircraft pilots who owe their skill to the instruction of air ace Tommy Rose who was at one time chief instructor and manager at Sywell.

A former flight-lieutenant in the R.A.F. he accounted for more than a dozen enemy aircraft during the First World War and was awarded the D.F.C. He became a national hero after breaking the outward and inward Cape record, the former beating Amy Johnson's solo flight by over thirteen hours. He was also a winner of the King's Cup air race and at the age of fifty-three won the Manx Air Derby. Among his many pupils at Sywell was popular stage and film actress Faith Bennett, seen here, who under the name of Margaret Riddick was a member of Northampton Repertory Company for a time.

219. S. P. Tyzack was also an early member of Northamptonshire Aero Club.

220. Lord Willoughby de Broke was Chairman of Sywell Aerodrome prior to the Second World War.

221. Lord Willoughby de Broke gave a flying party at Sywell in May, 1933. Seated round the table, clockwise from foreground: Colonel G. S. Eunson (President, Northampton Chamber of Commerce), Miss Ruth Nicholson, Mr F. Heycock, Miss Margarete von Treskow, Mr W. Lindsay Everard, M.P., Mrs G. S. Eunson, Lord Willoughby de Broke, Princess Mathilde Windisch-Graetz and three unidentified visitors.

222. Four celebrities at Northamptonshire Aero Club dinner held in Northampton Town Hall, 1935. Left to right: Ken Waller, Lord Willoughby de Broke, C. W. A. Scott and Captain G. R. D. Shaw.

223. The Annual Dinner of the 4th Battalion Northamptonshire Regiment, 1934.

The personalities are (left to right, seated): Colonel G. S. Eunson, Earl Spencer, Colonel H. N. Scott-Robson, Colonel R. Howlett, Colonel R. M. Raynsford. (Second row): Lieutenant D. M. Dorr, Lieutenant R. A. Palmer, Lieutenant F. M. Beers, Major E. Coley, Colonel Sir John Brown, Major L. E. Barnes, Captain D. J. Jelley, 2nd Lieutenant P. B. Heap, 2nd Lieutenant D. G. King. (Back row): Captain D. E. Taunton, Quartermaster F. G. Bowtell, Captain J. H. Johnson, Captain A. J. Yates, Lieutenant W. H. Langford.

225. *Below.* D. G. (later Sir Donald) Bradman who headed the Australian team that played at the County Ground, surrounded by admiring nurses at Manfield Hospital. He and other Australian players visited the hospital in August 1930 to cheer up the crippled boys in a Scout troop which had been formed there.

224. Northamptonshire cricket history was made in 1954 when fast bowler Frank Tyson and wicket-keeper Keith Andrew were chosen for the England touring team of Australia.

Frank is seen here, a lone figure on Northampton station, waiting for a London train to take him on the first leg of the journey. He was to become a national hero as the world's fastest bowler earning him the nickname of 'Typhoon' Tyson. He played in fourteen tests, taking forty-six wickets.

226. Some Wimbledon 'cracks' outside the former home of the Paget family at Sulby. Mr and Mrs F. A. Pearson gave a pre-Wimbledon party at their beautiful old house (now demolished) at Sulby in Northamptonshire.

The photograph shows (left to right, behind): M. S. Rodzianko (Russian champion), H. Cochet and M. Bernard (Junior champion, France). (Front Row): Frau Prenn, Mlle. Goldsmidt, Mlle. Rosambert, Mr F. A. Pearson, Mme. Cochet, Dr. Prenn (German champion) and M. Plaa (World's champion professional).

227. The ball speeds past the keeper's outstretched fingers in this Cobblers v Coventry match at the County Ground in Northampton, in September 1956.

228. The New Theatre 'Come to the Show' girls donned 'Cobblers' colours when they visited the County Ground.

229. Former Arsenal and England football star Tommy Lawton with his family after the christening of his son at Barton Seagrave, near Kettering. His goal scoring talents were greeted with roars of approval by vast crowds of soccer fans. In 1956-7 he became manager of Kettering Town F.C. taking them to the Southern League Championship. In 1955 Northampton spectators were able to see him in action in the first local floodlit match which took place at the British Timken ground at Duston in aid of charity.

230. The Peterborough Show saw the Gloucesters out in force. Left, looking pensive, is the Duke, while the Duchess chats with show president Lord Brassey. Prince William is standing. Prince Richard peers through railings on the right.

231. King George VI and Queen Elizabeth visited Silverstone races in 1950. The photograph shows the Queen and Earl Howe, Chairman of the stewards, touring the pits. Following is Princess Margaret.

233. The ageing King in 1950. He was to die of lung cancer in February 1951.

232. Contrasts in a King. The youthful Duke of York (later King George VI) at a meet in the 1930s.

234. Stock car racing at Brafield stadium.

235. Bertram Mills, owner of the famous circus, with his family at a local gymkhana.

236. Barbara Cartland (sitting second from left) was a guest of the family and directors of McCorquodale of Wolverton (printers) in October 1946.

237. Haggis is served at a Burns' Night dinner to Mrs Cowper Barrons. On her right is her husband, President of Northampton Town and County Scottish Association; on her left Mr Henderson Stewart, M.P. The Piper is Corporal Piper Smith of the 1st Battalion Scots Guards.

238. Tom Osborne Robinson, scenic designer for the Royal Theatre from 1928 to 1975, presents a painting to Northampton Art Gallery 'for the children of Northampton'. In the background is Alderman John Poole, Mayor of Northampton in 1969, and later (1977-81) Chairman of the County Council. Tom Robinson was a designer of national reputation, occasionally designing for the Royal Shakespeare Company.

239. 'Royal Occasion'—a Coronation exhibition, 28 February—28 March 1953, at Northampton Museum and Art Gallery. Celebrated stage and screen actress Freda Jackson (Mrs Henry Bird) talks to the curator, Reginald Brown. All the photographs displayed are by Roland Holloway.

240. Celebrities at a charity film show at the Exchange cinema in Northampton in 1933. From the left: the Hon. Mrs and Captain Reginald Macdonald-Buchanan, Lady Hardy, Lady Cromwell, Mrs M. Borwick, the Hon. Nancy Alsop, Sir Rupert Hardy, Lord Cromwell and the Hon. Mrs and Colonel J. G. Lowther.

241. The Northampton Naturist Club photographed at a former tennis club ground in Freehold Street at the back of Barratt's shoe factory. About a hundred nudists of all ages and sizes were either playing badminton, relaxing around the court or taking refreshment in the pavilion.

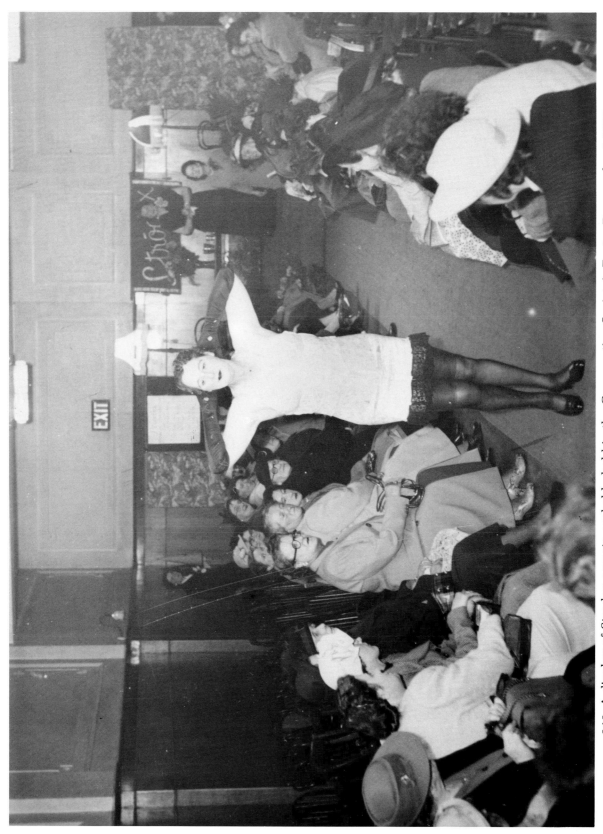

242. A display of Strodex corsets probably held in the Co-operative Society's Exeter Rooms, about 1938.

243-4. Fashion parade, modern style, probably at Adnitt Brothers (now Debenhams) in Northampton. The mannequin in the top photograph was a Vietnamese student at the Northampton School of Art, St. George's Avenue.

245. A Grenadier Guards' dinner to which lady guests were invited was held at Kettering in 1933. In the front row are Colonel G. E. C. Rasch (who commanded the Grenadiers), Lady Burghley, Lord Burghley, M.P., Major-General Lord Loch and Mr A. N. P. Andrews.

246. Comedian Sid James gives film star Janette Scott a kiss at a jazz festival at Northampton Drill Hall in November 1964.

247. Tom Walls (with moustache) at a charity Ball at Franklin's Gardens, in aid of the Cancer Campaign. Tom was born in Byron Street, Northampton and attended a Kingsley school. He embarked on a stage career which was later to include the popular Aldwych farces. Among many films was the *Blarney Stone* which had its world premiere at the Exchange cinema. It was screened to packed houses every night. A keen member of the Pytchley Hunt, he took a cottage in Chapel Brampton for the season and a film episode was 'shot' in the locality. During this period Tom visited the Towcester races several times, usually when he had a horse running.

248. Here he is seen at the 1933 premiere of *The Old Dark House* at the Exchange cinema with staff, including Mr 'Pat' Thornton, manager for many years. A life-long ambition was fulfilled in 1932 when his horse April V won the Derby at 100-6. He died in 1949.

250. Errol Flynn arrives at Sywell Aerodrome in 1954 when he opened a Repertory Company garden party at Boughton Hall. With him are his third wife Patrice Wymore (left) and Freda Jackson (Mrs Henry Bird) who was in the Company when he was a member of it.

249. *Opposite*. Ben Lyon and his wife Bebe Daniels were in Northampton in 1938. Here they take tea in the former Derngate café, now the site of part of the Derngate Centre.

251. Film stars Moore Marriott (the Old Man) and Graham Moffatt (the Fat Boy). They were celebrated for their characterisations in the Will Hay films. Marriott lived at Everdon and served on Daventry Council. Moffatt ran a hotel at Braybrooke.

252. A gentle giant. The photograph shows Dutch giant Jan Van Albert who was appearing at the New Theatre, Northampton. He is being shown round the town by photographer Roland Holloway, of average height. (*Chronicle and Echo*)

253. Prizewinners David Simons and Anthony Harris
at a Pitsford baby show in 1935.

EVENTS

254. The 1925 historical pageant held in Abington Park, Northampton.

255. Part of the Northampton Carnival Parade of 1937 proceeding up Gold Street into George Row. In front is an elaborately decorated lorry portraying the musical 'Show Boat' which won a Championship Cup for John White Ltd. of Rushden. Note the police box in the centre of the road for traffic control.

256. Beckett and Sargeant charity school prizegiving in 1932. The prizes were presented by the Mayor, Alderman C. J. Scott.

257. The Duke of York opens the new College of Technology in St. George's Avenue, Northampton in 1932.

Others in the picture (left to right) are the Duchess of York, now the Queen Mother, Mr E. Bordoli, Mr A. H. Hollister, Councillor S. Strickland, Mr W. J. Parker, Mr C. G. B. Allinson and Councillor J. Peach.

258. Miss Monica Stokes of Northampton became the County's first Shoe Trade Queen in 1935. She rode in the Carnival procession in a huge gold shoe.

259. Air Chief Marshal Sir Philip Joubert unveils a plaque over the main entrance of Northampton Grammar School in Billing Road as part of the quater-centenary celebrations. They had been delayed from 1941 to June 1947 due to the war.

Thomas Chipsey, a grocer assigned lands at Holcot, Pitsford and Far Cotton for the endowment of a free school and at the start it was housed in old premises near Marefair (formerly St. Gregory's Church) in what was later named Freeschool Street. The headmaster was paid a salary of £9 a year, with one teacher and one usher. Lessons began at 6 a.m., unpunctuality being punished by a beating. A new era dawned in 1867 when lessons were held in the old Corn Exchange (later a cinema). Then came a move to Abington Square on a site now occupied by the A.B.C. cinema, where a building had been constructed for £3,000 to accommodate two hundred pupils; it was opened in 1870. When the accommodation became inadequate, the governors decided to build a new one on Billing Road. This was completed in 1911 at a cost of £16,000.

260. The masters of the Grammar School (now the Northampton School for Boys) in 1947.

Seated from left: D. C. Foster, H. J. Smith, R. W. Hollowell, T. C. Lees, B. A. Swindon, Dr. E. E. Field, M. B. Nettleton, headmaster, A. M. Walmsley, A. T. Davies, W. Peach, D. J. Evans, E. R. Hughes and R. Richardson-Jones, music master. *Middle Row:* D. H. King, J. H. Arnold, D. C. Johnstone, S. Buchwalter, H. L. Harris, G. Moss, A. R. H. Stebbing, H. N. Lance, G. C. Pether, R. V. P. Adams, E. B. Johnson, O. W. Layzell and J. P. Mounsey. *Back Row:* P. Ambridge, C. A. Richmond, F. H. Trotter, S. Weindling, D. E. Gommon, J. G. Leitch, L. Duckett, D. Young, D. B. Gregor and R. Bonnichon.

261. The Mounts Baths, Northampton were built at a cost of £52,500 on the site of the old gaol and opened in 1936 by former Olympic hurdles champion Lord Burghley, seen in the centre of this group. He later inherited the title of Marquess of Exeter. Following the opening 10,127 people paid a visit of inspection in one day.

Others in the group, from left, are the Mayor (Councillor S. Perkins), Lady Burghley, Councillor W. J. Bassett-Lowke, the Mayoress (Mrs Perkins), the Mayor of Hastings (Councillor E. Ford), Alderman A. Burrows, the Town Clerk (Mr W. R. Kew), Mrs A. Burrows, the Mayoress of Hastings and builder Mr H. A. Glenn.

262. A procession arriving at Memorial Square, Northampton for the opening in September 1951.
From the right: The Mayor (Councillor Frank Lee), the Marquess of Exeter (Lord Lieutenant), the Marchioness of Exeter, Mr W. R. Kew (Borough Freeman), the Mayoress (Mrs Lee), Mr R. T. Paget, M.P., Alderman A. L. Chown, Alderman Mrs H. M. Nicholls and Alderman Len Smith. The garden which is dedicated to the fallen of World War II stands on a site once occupied by St. Katharine's Church. The site escaped the re-development plan for the area, and now serves as an oasis in a desert of traffic and commerce.

264. *Below.* The statue arrives at Abington Park Museum courtyard awaiting its new siting in Delapre Park.

263. *Left.* Professor Frank Dobson, standing on the right, addresses the assembled townsfolk at the unveiling of his statue *Woman with Fish* in Memorial Square, Northampton in May 1952. The sculpture was vandalised, and after losing its head was removed to a Corporation depot, where it languished until a new home was found for it in Delapre Park.

265. One of the last horse-drawn vehicles to be seen in the streets of Northampton was what was known as the Sheriff's coach, withdrawn from use in 1939. It was used for many years to convey the presiding judge at Northamptonshire Assizes to and from All Saints Church for the traditional service preceding the opening. It was owned by Mr John Frisby who together with his brother Bob had stables at the former Peacock Hotel in the Market Square.

266. Members of Northampton Board of Guardians assembled in the forecourt of the Public Assistance Institution, Wellingborough Road in 1932, to witness a planting of two weeping elm trees in memory of deceased members of the board, Alderman A. G. Slinn and Mrs C. S. Wilson. The planting was performed by Councillor James Jackson holding spade, and the Mayor, Alderman C. J. Scott next to him with the Mayoress, Mrs R. H. Stone.

267. November 1932, and the Duke of York and his Duchess, now the Queen Mother, pay an official visit to Northampton. The Duke opened the new College of Technology (see illustration no. 257) and the Duchess the John Greenwood Shipman Home at Dallington.

268. Mr John Williamson, a former Chief Constable of Northampton,
speaking at a local garden party.

On 5 November 1930, Alfred Arthur Rouse, a London commercial traveller, murdered an unknown man by hitting him on the head in Hardingstone Lane, leaving him in Rouse's car, which the murderer set alight. Convicted at the Assizes, Northampton, Rouse was hanged at Bedford Gaol on 10 March 1931.

269. The Rouse murder car. The car was gutted, but the number plate is plain to see.

270. The grave of the victim in Hardingstone church yard.

271. Police searching a hedgerow near the scene. A mallet was found.

272. The traditional ceremony of reading the Proclamation of the Queen's accession to the throne took place in Northampton Market Square in February 1952, and the Mayor, Councillor Frank Lee is seen reading it from the steps of the iron fountain.

Also seen on the left are the Mayor's Sergeant, Mr W. F. Floyd, holding the mace; Alderman Cyril Chown; the Town Clerk, Mr C. E. Vivian Rowe; the Town Hall Keeper, Mr Sam Furniss; the Chief Fire Officer, Mr Arthur Spence, and Major (later Lieutenant-Colonel) J. T. Ennalls, CO of Simpson Barracks. On the right are the High Sheriff, Captain G. W. M. Lees; the Mayoress, Mrs Lee; Alderman Mrs H. M. Nicholls, and other members of the Town Council.

273. Grammar School boys listen to the reading of the Proclamation.

274. On Sunday, 15 April 1962, demolition day arrived for Northampton's old cast iron fountain which had occupied pride of place on the Market Square since it was donated to the town by Captain Samuel Isaac in 1863.

Coronation Day on 2 June 1953 started with ceremonial parades, civic and military services on Northampton Market Square and other small events, but it was in the terraced streets later in the day that loyal citizens held their own festivities—the culmination of many weeks of saving and preparation. Flags and bunting were in evidence everywhere, all ages mingled round heavily laden tea-tables positioned down the centre of roads. What few television owners there were, kept 'open house' for those who wished to see the broadcast pictures. There were prizes for sports, fancy dress and other competitions, but a hush descended at 9 o'clock as all listened to the voice of the newly crowned Queen. 15,750 local school children received coronation mugs and old people also received gifts. The celebrations were completed with a fireworks display.

275. There were flags in plenty around Northampton on Coronation Day, but none so obscure as this patriotic gesture fluttering amid a maze of old rooftops and chimney pots at the rear of premises in Sheep Street.

276. Children from the Mounts district with their own 'Queen and Duke'.

277. Coronation Day party in Albert Street. It was later demolished and now lies beneath the Grosvenor Centre.

278. Coronation Day, in Gladstone Terrace, a small cul-de-sac just off Barrack Road. It consisted of just forty-four houses and was noted for its community spirit. In the last war one hundred and twenty-four men joined the Forces and of these twenty-four died. On Coronation Day a canopy of flags and bunting gained it a major prize in the best decorated street competition. It was known as Northampton's version of Coronation Street. The terrace was demolished in 1966.

279.
Coronation
Day in the
closing room
of J. Sears
and Co.
shoe factory,
Northampton.

280. Coronation Day. Children gather in Thornton Park, Kingsthorpe.

281. Coronation Day. Maypole dancing at Harpole.

282. One of the first County branches of the Women's Institute was formed at Great Houghton in 1917 and others quickly followed. The headquarters consisted of a small room and use of another in Marefair which proved totally inadequate for the ever-expanding movement. Consequently it came as a relief in May 1958 when the new W.I. House was opened in Albion Place, Northampton. The ceremony was performed by the Duchess of Gloucester (Princess Alice) who is seen on the right of the picture moving among some of the two hundred members present. With her is the Hon. Mrs G. T. H. Capron, the then County Chairman; following are the Mayor (Councillor V. J. H. Harris) and the Hon. Mrs Macdonald-Buchanan.

283. High Sheriff Sir Evelyn Fanshawe heads the Assize procession from All Saints Church in 1960.

284. A Corporation luncheon in Northampton Town Hall in 1950 for Councillors and Council officials.

285. Employees of the *Chronicle and Echo* at an 'After the War' dinner in Northampton Town Hall in 1947.

286. Alderman John Poole becomes Mayor of the County Borough of Northampton in 1969; looking on is the Town Clerk, Mr Alan Parkhouse; on the right is Alderman Ruth Perkins, Mayor in 1968.

287. Newly elected Mayor, Alderman B. P. C. Sheppard, installs his wife as Mayoress in Brackley Town Hall in 1967. Town Clerk Mr J. Wild smiles with approval.

288. A strike meeting at the Duston British Timken works in January 1960.

289. Accident between an Austin Seven and a delivery van. The Austin had cable operated front-wheel brakes. Note the petrol tank just in front of the dash-board.

290. A lorry sheds its load on the Weedon Road in Northampton.

291. A fifty-ton tractor crashes into a house at Lamport, near the level crossing.

292. Roland Holloway's eye for the incongruous seldom deserted him.

293-5. Anti-nuclear demonstrators arrested in Wood Hill, Northampton in 1962. In the background of the above photograph is the *Black Boy Hotel*, remembered for its excellent lunches. It was demolished in 1963 to make way for a new Midland Bank building.

296. Recruits at a passing out parade at Simpson Barracks lose their hats in a gust of wind.

297. Firefighting at a farm at Brackley.

CHURCH AND CHAPEL

298. A view of St. Giles' Church, Northampton, from the General Hospital.

299. The Norman west door of St. Giles' Church has been described as 'a precious medieval relic' and is similar to the style used in Caen Cathedral, Normandy. The church, built around 1150, was originally outside the town walls. It was used for centuries for meetings of the Common Assembly and the election of Mayors and Bailiffs.

300. For many years the pupils of Beckett and Sargeant's School could be seen wearing their distinctive school uniform of white starched bonnet with cape and apron. The school was founded in 1735 by two local ladies, Dame Dorothy Beckett and Mistress Ann Sargeant, who left money for the endowment and maintenance of a school for thirty girls in the parish of All Saints; the girls marched in procession to the church every Sunday. The funds are now used for other educational purposes, but the original school building still stands at the top of Kingswell Street. In 1935 a 200th anniversary was held with a pageant depicting episodes over the period of its history.

301. 'The 29th of May is Oak Apple Day' and is observed in the traditional manner at All Saints Church, Northampton. Mr R. Ellis, the verger, is seen about to place an oak leaf garland on the statue of King Charles II over the portico. After the Great Fire of Northampton in 1675, the King granted 1,000 tons of timber from the royal forests of Whittlebury and Salcey, and seven years' remission of chimney tax money, for the rebuilding of All Saints.

302. The tower of Northampton's 'Mother Church' of All Saints has been a landmark for centuries. Here it is seen floodlit as part of the National Faraday celebrations of 1931 to honour the famous scientist. The black lines across the picture are overhead cables supplying current to the tramway system which was replaced by 'buses shortly afterwards.

303. *Opposite*. A wedding in All Saints Church during the 1930s.

304. A lone passer-
by pauses beneath
the portico of All
Saints Church.

305. The Roman Catholic Bishop of Northampton, the Rt. Rev. Mgr. Charles Grant being formally enthroned at the Cathedral, Barrack Road, in 1967.

306. Mgr. C. A. Grant, the new Bishop of Northampton.

307. Children watch Cardinal Godfrey, Archbishop of Westminster, enter Northampton Roman Catholic Cathedral for High Mass.

308. Tranquillity outside the Catholic Cathedral.

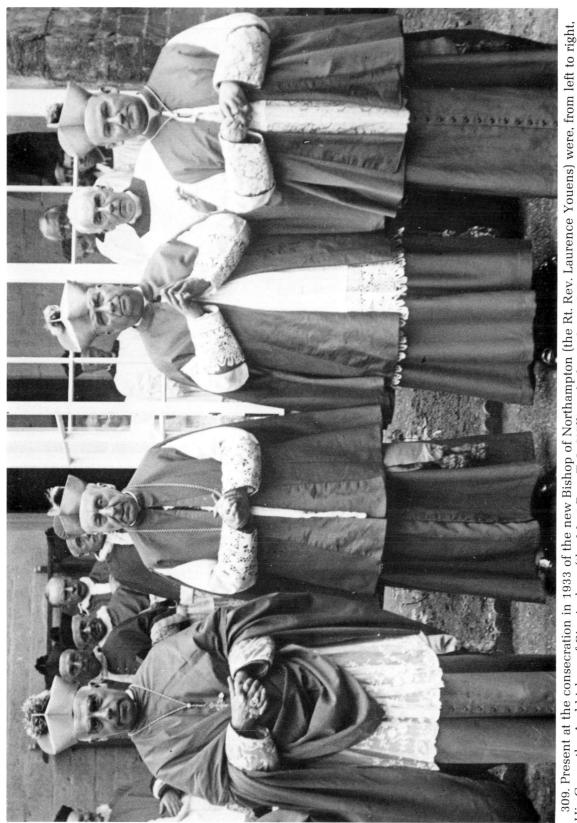

309. Present at the consecration in 1933 of the new Bishop of Northampton (the Rt. Rev. Laurence Youens) were, from left to right, His Grace the Archbishop of Birmingham (the Most Rev. T. L. Williams); the Bishop of Cambysopolis (the Rt. Rev. J. Butt); the Bishop of Northampton; Father Squirrel, M.C. to the Bishop; and the Bishop of Nottingham (the Rt. Rev. J. McNulty).

310. Interior of St. Matthew's Church, Northampton, some time in the 1930s. The church was built by Pickering Phipps in memory of his father, founder of Phipps Brewery, and a Northampton M.P., to the design of Matthew Holding, a Northampton architect. It was consecrated in 1893.

312. Two sisters sit in Notre Dame gardens. The chapel is in the background.

311. The chapel of Notre Dame, Northampton. There was widespread concern when it was announced that a firm of developers had acquired the premises formerly occupied by the Northampton Notre Dame High School, the Convent adjoining, a magnificent chapel, and peaceful gardens extending as far back as Lady's Lane. The Convent and School were built in 1871 with extensions to the latter being added in 1938; it included an assembly hall to seat five hundred, with a stage and modern lighting. The chapel was opened in 1881 with its fine stained glass windows and carvings. An attempt to save it was made by the Action Group who applied to the Environmental Minister for it to be 'listed' and converted into a museum, Chapel of Rest or concert hall. The gardens, it was claimed, would form one of the most beautiful precincts in the town centre for shoppers who thronged Abington Street only a few yards away. However the bid failed. There was a preservation order on some trees but this did not save them when bulldozers moved in on a Sunday morning in April 1979, razing the Chapel and uprooting most of the garden. The School is now situated at Moulton Park; a reminder of the Chapel, in the form of a crucifix, hangs in St. Gregory's Roman Catholic Church, Park Avenue North.

314. The boy 'bishop' at Earls Barton Church. In the centre is the Reverend Louis Ewart, Vicar from 1930 to 1958.

313. *Opposite.* A team of bellringers herald in the New Year at the Church of the Holy Sepulchre in Northampton, one of only four remaining 'round' churches in England. There is a peal of eight bells, the two oldest dated 1681; two trebles were added in 1897 in commemoration of Queen Victoria's diamond jubilee. In 1926 the old oak beams supporting the bells were found to be infected by death watch beetle and were replaced by a steel frame; at the same time all except one of the 1681 bells were recast.

315. An ancient custom revived at Earls Barton Church. Monks preached from the same tower over one thousand years ago. It also served as a look-out. The service is being conducted by the Reverend Louis Ewart.

316. A joke is appreciated by clergymen, some of 230 from Northamptonshire, who attended a five-day convention at Oxford, arranged by the Bishop of Peterborough.

317. The Bishop of Peterborough, the Rt. Rev. Cyril Eastaugh, listens to the reading of the Mandate soon after entering Peterborough Cathedral for his enthronement in January 1962.

ANIMALS

318. Orphan lamb and foster mother at a Paulerspury farm.

319. Bloodhound pups.

320. Shooting trophies presented to Abington Museum by the late Mr R. B. Loder of Maidwell. In the centre is Mr Reginald Brown, curator.

322. A welcome drink of lemonade at a horse show and gymkhana.

321. *Left*. A winning pair at the County Show.

323. Sheepdog demonstration in Abington Park.

324. Another winner at the County Show.

326. An African Crane, photographed by Roland Holloway whilst on holiday at Paignton.

325. *Opposite.* The small boy lived on the same Northamptonshire farm as this champion of a British Timken Show. The show was discontinued in 1978.

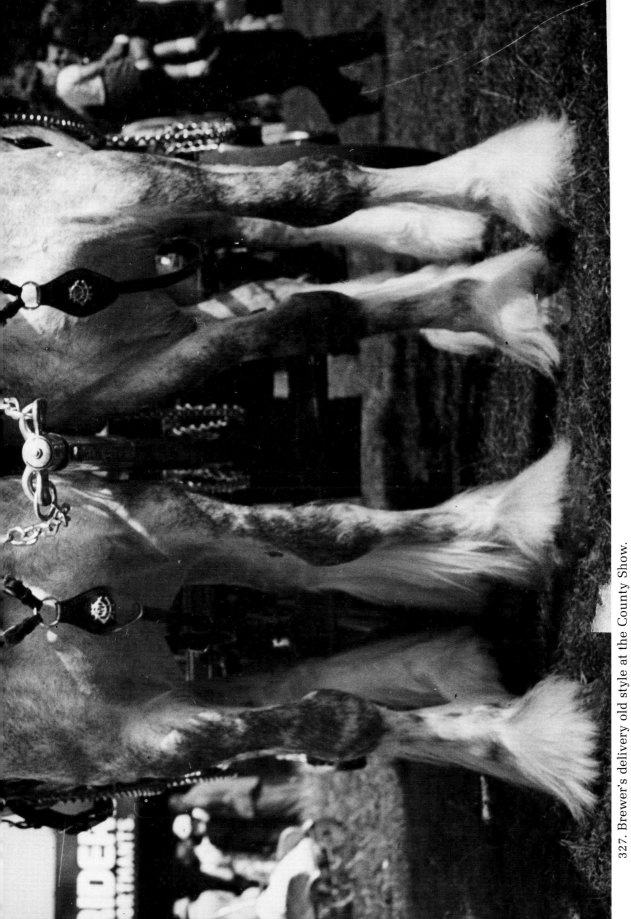

327. Brewer's delivery old style at the County Show.

329-30. Dogs and owners at Northampton Drill Hall in 1969.

328. *Opposite.* St. Bernards *Sally* and *Cherry* at a dog show at Northampton Drill Hall in 1969.

331-2. Pets' cemeteries are something of a rarity but there is one, now discontinued, in the grounds of the Co-operative Society Funeral Service in Barrack Road, Northampton. The Elwes family also had one in Billing Hall Park.

333-6. When Wellingborough Zoo Park opened in 1945 it quickly became a major attraction. It closed in 1970 and some of the animals were disposed of by public auction. A lioness fetched £45, a pair of tawny eagles £22, whilst a goat fetched £10, bought by a Northampton man 'to keep the grass down'. Surprisingly the highest price was £84 paid for two penguins.

337. Swans at South Bridge, Northampton.

338. British beef at the Northamptonshire Agricultural Show.

WEATHER HAZARDS

339. An Austin van belonging to the Farmers Supply Association (butchers), in St. Giles Square, Northampton, about 1936. Cleaning the windscreen is S. C. Amos.

340. Winter on Wood Hill, Northampton.

341. Northampton Market Square. The fountain was demolished in 1962.

342. Becket's Park, Northampton.

343. Bleak outlook for a goat at Northampton cattle market.

344. Feeding sheep near Wootton.

345. Outside the *Dog and Duck* in Wellingborough in 1939.

346. Office workers are ferried across the main road during floods at St. James', Northampton in 1939.

347. Smiling employees at Whitworth's Mill, Wellingborough are rescued by boat; others await their turn on the steps.

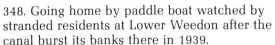

348. Going home by paddle boat watched by stranded residents at Lower Weedon after the canal burst its banks there in 1939.

349. *Above, right.* Northampton cattle market in 1939, when flood water caused the evacuation of cattle, and cars were abandoned in over three feet of water.

350. Two soldiers on leave stranded in their car at Kislingbury in 1939.

351. One of Northampton's heaviest falls of snow occurred in 1947.
Here youngsters dig themselves a passage in Windmill Terrace.

OUT IN THE COUNTY: AND BEYOND

352. Blossom time at Orlingbury.

353. *Opposite.* Misty morning on a Northamptonshire farm in the 1930s.

354. *Right.* The Northamptonshire College of Agriculture, Moulton is opened in May 1935 by the Minister of Agriculture, Mr Walter Elliot. He is about to unlock the main door with a silver key. Also seen are the benefactor Mrs A. S. Harrison, Mrs Walter Elliot, Mr J. M. Eady, Chairman of the County Council Agriculture Committee, and Mr W. A. Stewart, College Principal.

355. Flax harvesting at Cold Ashby.

358. A spot of demolition that went wrong. The 200 year-old oak tree at Overstone Park should have fallen to the left, but instead it came towards the camera. There was just time for Roland Holloway to press the shutter before he took to his heels.

356. *Opposite, above.* Storm clouds over Harlestone Heath.

357. *Opposite.* Rural beauty in Northamptonshire, photographed from the main Northampton-Welford road overlooking Hollowell reservoir.

359. Anne, second wife of Roland Holloway, beside the canal at Blisworth.

360. Rural scene at Milton Malsor.

361. Viaduct at Lower Weedon.

362. *Below left.* Inside the two-mile-long canal tunnel between Stoke Bruerne and Blisworth. It was closed from 1979 to 1984 for urgent reconstruction work to be carried out.

363. Bargees off for a canal honeymoon at Stoke Bruerne in 1937. Mr William Blackman and his bride had lived all their lives on barges.

364. Autumn sunset—the approach to Wellingborough from Finedon.

365.

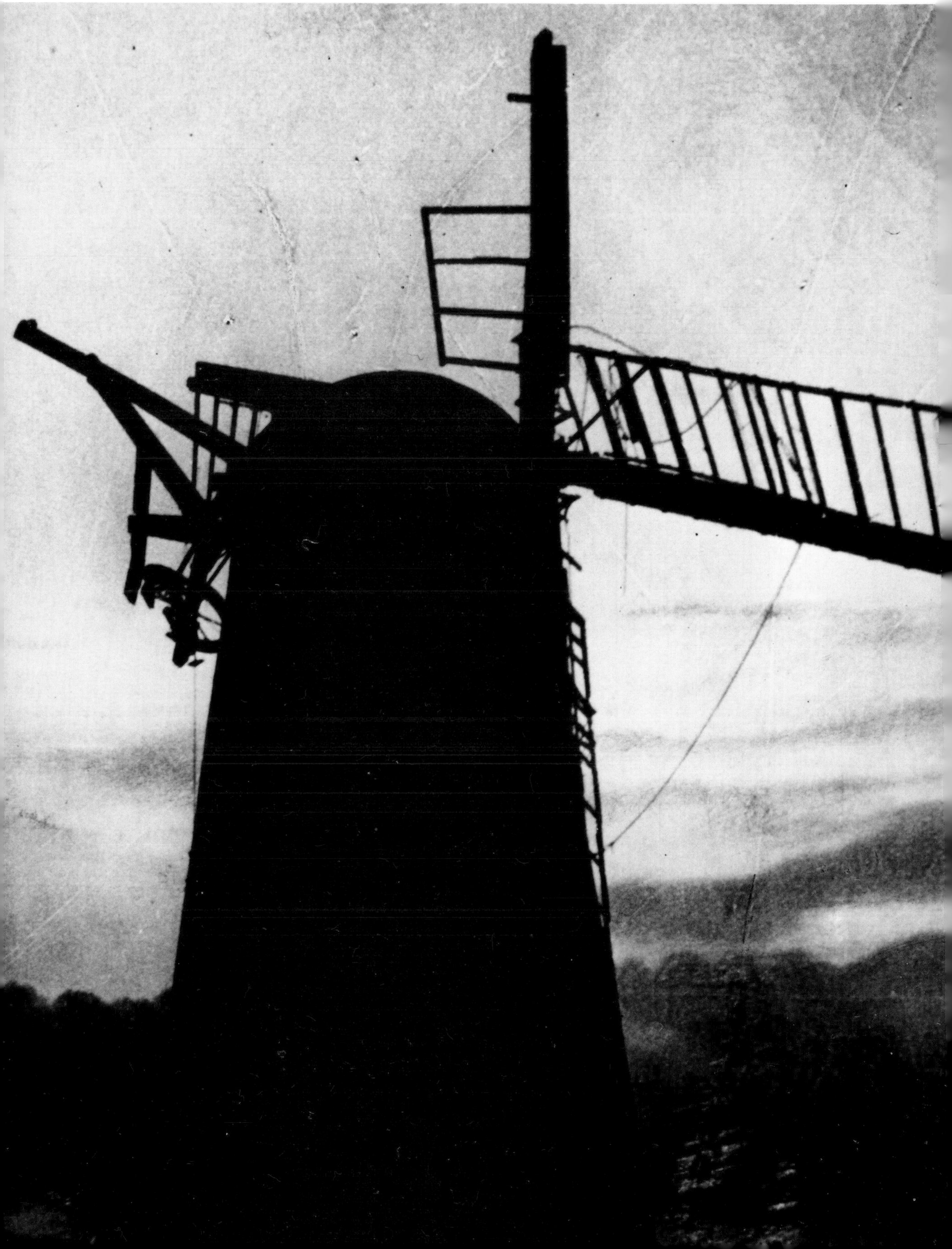

Windmills were once a familiar sight all over Northamptonshire, but today almost all have disappeared. However a few still exist in some shape or form, and on the outskirts of Northampton can be seen the remains of two, minus the sails, converted into part of residential properties. Passing through Wootton on a summer evening in 1935, Roland Holloway obtained (*left*) this sunset picture of the mill there in its final stages of decay. It has since undergone a chequered history having been used as a water tower, an observation post for the Home Guard during the Second World War, and finally (*below*) part of a modern home surrounded by a flower garden and lawn. Another conversion can be seen (*right*) in the appropriately named Windmill Terrace, Kingsthorpe. The stone walls are three feet thick at its base, the whole being warm in winter and cool in summer. A winding staircase leads to the bedrooms and a flat roof which provides a commanding view of the town. In 1900 Mr T. Wilson, founder of the building firm purchased the mill and lived there, and a son Mr Con Wilson was born there.

366. Converted windmill, Kingsthorpe.

367. Wootton windmill converted into part of a modern residence.

368. The village of Boughton has a church but it also had a predecessor standing about half-a-mile away in ruins. Scheduled as an ancient monument, it dates from the fourteenth century or even earlier, and takes its name from St. John the Baptist. A service is held there once a year, the congregation sitting among the gravestones and the almost completely overgrown masonry.

Here the service is being taken by the Archdeacon of Northampton (the Venerable C. F. Knyvett) in the late 1930s. It is believed that the church fell into gradual disuse after the people of Old Boughton fled at the time of the Black Death of 1349. The last service inside was a wedding in 1708, and for centuries Boughton Green Fair was held in a field adjacent to it.

369. The former Althorp Park railway station standing in isolation—a contrast to the days when it was decorated and crowds would assemble in the forecourt. It was built in 1881, closed in 1960 and subsequently demolished in 1962, after seeing more royalty and other notabilities pass through its portals than all the other County stations combined.

In the early days there would be a pair-horse Brougham waiting to convey visitors to the Spencers' stately seat of Althorp half-a-mile distant. On one occasion there was the Empress of Russia and her sister Queen Alexandra of Denmark guarded by a giant Russian officer with a brace of pistols stuck in his belt. The railway company allowed the Earls Spencer to have a private waiting room appropriately furnished and the privilege of allowing trains to be specially stopped for the family. A grim link with the McRae murder in 1892 was provided when the woman victim's torso was found in a sack nearby.

370. The County has close associations with the conspirators of the Gunpowder Plot when Guy Fawkes and his companions sought to 'blow the King and Parliament all up alive'.

The real villains of the piece were the conceiver and the betrayer, both of them Northamptonshire men. It was in 1603 that Robert Catesby of Ashby St. Ledgers first conceived the plot, and secret meetings were held in the oak-timbered building seen in the picture. Catesby was the driving force who leased a house next to the Houses of Parliament and packed the cellars with explosive. In 1605 all was ready, but fate intervened when Francis Tresham of Rushton Hall wrote an anonymous letter exposing the plan. Robert Catesby made a frantic dash on horseback from London covering eighty miles in four hours to bring news that the plot had been discovered.

371. One would hardly associate this picturesque little country cottage with crime, yet in 1952 it was the scene of an horrific double murder, which engaged the Northamptonshire police in one of the most puzzling mysteries in the County's criminal history.

A delivery boy on his rounds at the quiet little village of Ashton, near Oundle, not getting the customary answer to knocks went for help, when it was discovered that the elderly occupants had been brutally murdered. Mr Harry Peach, 64, was found battered to death in one room and his wife dying from massive injuries in another; she died in hospital later without being able to make a statement. Scotland Yard were called in and months of inquiries were conducted including some 1,500 interviews, 600 detailed statements and 800 people, including the entire male population of Ashton, fingerprinted.

372. County Police chiefs confer at the scene of the Ashton double killing.

373. Rows of skulls and bones in the bone crypt beneath the church at Rothwell.

375. In the foreground are Northamptonshire delegates to the Women's Institute two day Annual General Meeting at the Albert Hall, here seen at lunch break on the steps of the Albert Memorial.

374. *Left.* This 'bird's eye view' shows a section of a vast gathering of over 5,000 women at the Annual General Meeting of Women's Institutes in the Royal Albert Hall, London.

376. Speech Day in the grounds of Stowe School, Buckinghamshire.

377. Tyringham House, Buckinghamshire.

378. Burghley House in Lincolnshire remains one of the largest and grandest surviving buildings of the Elizabethan age.

THE PHOTOGRAPHER AT WORK

The photographer reflected as he photographs an event in Northampton's old Masonic Hall.

Below: Hazardous work from the top of Northampton's Market Square fountain.

Roland Holloway wrote the following before his death.

In these days of automatic cameras it is interesting to recall those early days when equipment consisted of a solid half-plate camera, a dozen slides (glass plate holders), collapsible tripod and a black cloth under which the photographer's head disappeared for focusing. The flashlight apparatus consisted of magnesium powder, percussion caps (as used in toy pistols), and a metal tray with a handle on which the powder was sprinkled. The spark from the percussion cap would ignite the powder (but not always) which would send up a mushroom of dense smoke. Another method was introduced whereby the powder was ignited by a wheel and flint, which in turn was superseded by bulbs containing magnesium foil, fired from a battery in the handle of a large plated reflector. Even this system, whilst being cleaner and more reliable, had its hazards, for sometimes a bulb would explode scattering glass in all directions—especially dangerous for close-up pictures. The problem was solved later by coating the bulbs.

Roland Holloway developed his own synchro-flash mechanism in 1930. It was made with the aid of wire, electrical fittings and a cycle-lamp battery.

Bill Linney and Gerald and Roland Holloway on wedding duty.

land Holloway (second from right) on duty at a Salvation Army rally in rthampton Market Square.

The 'King of the kids' ready to photograph his favourite subject.

At Sywell Aerodrome.

Roland was an expert animal photographer.

The photographer takes a good vantage point at Northampton's Abington Park during a carnival parade.

INDEX

All numbers are illustration numbers

N = Northampton